AF347052

Songs of Suicide

Songs of Suicide

Onkar Sharma

HAWAKAL

hawakal

Published by Hawakal Publishers
185 Kali Temple Road, Nimta, Kolkata 700049
India

Email info@hawakal.com
Website www.hawakal.com

First edition July, 2020

Copyright © Onkar Sharma 2020

Cover image: Shutterstock
Cover design: Bitan Chakraborty

All rights reserved. No part of this publication may be reproduced or transmitted (other than for purposes of review/critique) in any form or by any means, electronic or mechanical, including photocopy, recording, or any information storage and retrieval system without prior permission in writing from the publisher or the copyright holder where applicable. The author asserts his moral right to be identified as the author of his work.

ISBN: 978-81-945273-1-2

Price: 200 INR | USD 8.99

For
my mother *Chanchala Devi*
and
father Late *Anant Ram*

ACKNOWLEDGEMENTS

Rita Sharma, my love and spouse. For being the support through thick and thin.

Elina Sharma, my little angel and daughter. For enlightening my life with her naughty and sneaky moves.

Rajeev Thakur, my friend. For encouraging me and believing in me unwaveringly.

Manoj Kumar, my teacher and guide. For showing the path and being the light.

Late *Desh Raj Pathania*, my teacher, mentor, guide and morale booster. For sowing the seeds of a writer in me.

CONTENTS

Introduction

The biggest reason why I felt driven to pen down this collection is my mother and her journey through a painful psychiatric condition. A patient of Acute Psychotic Disorder (APD), she has throughout her life until a decade back manifested suicidal behaviour. In my childhood I saw her attempting to jump off the balcony, trying to press her throat umpteenth times and searching for poisonous substances desperately. But the worst and the most horrible attempts she ever made were the ones when she tried to burn her head with kerosene. She tried this trick numerous times in her psychotic condition and mostly failed. But once she almost succeeded. It was the month of March in the middle of the night and I was asleep. The demon inhabiting her head prodded and incited her to soak her head with kerosene yet again. In no time, she set her head on fire.

With flames arising from the head, she ran hysterically crying her lungs out. Her screams from that attempt, which were also heard across the valley in faraway villages, still ring in my ears. The memory upsets me even today after so many years. Fortunate was I that the fire was extinguished in time with the help of my cousin, Vicky. We poured water on her head immediately. She sustained a few burns on the ear-side, which would heal eventually. From then on, she is on continuous medication, consulting a psychiatrist regularly and is perfectly okay.

I have noticed that when she is out of the psychotic state, she is progressive, forward-looking, foresighted, caring and sprightly. She doesn't even think of doing anything stupid like that.

Her psychotic condition taught me to empathize with people who find themselves ridden down the suicidal road. I wonder if they are souls enchanted by the beauty of death or they are minds controlled by parasitic spirits. These spirits may be the ones constantly instigating them to inflict self-harm.

Having seen several such lives, I realise that we don't have a right to question them, judge them or hurl incendiary remarks. It does not help. Rather it worsens the situation making the world uninhabitable for them. No one can understand what they have been through or their state of mind and the amount of depression they are buried under. We can only try to make them feel at ease so that they can open up about the deepest, otherwise-assumed shameful, suppressed fears or emotions. Allowing them to talk openly is the first step in subsiding their suicidal urge. People prone to suicide can be engaged in discussions. But there is a challenge. Often it is observed that a person, who resorts to extreme measure, barely leaves clues of dying. Such a person can be anyone. He/she may have watched a movie with us last night, or have had drinks with us a while back. Gauging and singling out the suicidal minds remain a puzzle, even for the experts.

Nevertheless, we can join elusive instances from the life of a suicidal personal and connect the dots. We have to read through the subtle hints, which he/she leaves around. Many psychologists insist on catching vital hints pointing out to a suicide. Dr Anjali Chhabria is one such who in her book '*Death Is Not The Answer*' records a few instances that can help us gather whether a person is trying to end up his/her life. She suggests that a person trying to wrap up his finances, reducing social contact, giving away personal possessions, rectifying past mistakes or regrets, among others, can be in a potential danger of committing suicide.[1] Dr Chhabria also insists that speaking quickly to such a fellow is of paramount importance. This can allow him/her a chance to express their hearts out alleviating them of the burden on their psyche. Sigmund Freud in his avant-garde work '*Psychoanalysis*'[2] was the first to propose the idea of bringing the unconscious thoughts, desires, memories and feelings into the conscious mind of people to relieve them from psychological disturbances and distresses. This is an effective tool to save a hopeless life. Maybe, we can succeed in saving this way an important life and cut down the count of 800,000, who, as per the World Health Organisation (WHO), every year globally die due to suicides.[3]

Through this collection I have touched upon the sensitive subject of 'suicide' with an aim to peep into the lives of people, who pass through atrocious circumstances and excruciating experiences so much so that suicide remains to them as the only choice. I chose poetry as a medium to fetch everybody's attention to this global pandemic – which is as contagious as COVID-19 and far more dangerous than any disease in the world. This might sound less lyrical. But the melody in the suicidal sadness, emptiness and loneliness will ring through the hearts of readers for a lot longer than can be imagined. I have worked a bit to add music to fictionalized anecdotes as well as incidents. This is the reason why I also call these songs as modern ballads. In short, this is a tribute to the troubled souls and, therefore, an effort to develop an understanding for the poor men and women whom we might have seen or heard of attempting to kill themselves.

Abundant employment of imagery to paint a genuine picture of the social-economic conditions, breaking away relations, mounting alienation in the age of social media, smartphones and digital channels came naturally to me.

Onkar Sharma

[1] Dr Anjali Chhabria's *Death Is Not The Answer*, Page No. 275 has written about 10 instances that can be signs of committing suicide.

[2] Sigmund Freud's *Psychoanalysis*

[3] The World Health Organisation's Suicide Data, Link: https://www.who.int/mental_health/prevention/suicide/suicideprevent/en/

Panchatatva — The Five Elements

i
the holy *jal*

he walked by the bridge-rail and mumbled.
he sobbed on his past mistakes and tumbled.
yet he held himself and stopped in the centre
to overlook at the eerie waves that did enter
in broad daylight through the discarded waste
and mired the abutments with stinking paste.

at the crossroads of life and death,
in search of liberty and boundlessness
combating within to beat the outside world
fired executive leaned over the bridge
and looked at the waves - black and purple;
and looked at his life that'd turned turtle.
'bankloan and emis must sink in there.
the curse of credit cards must end here,"
he mumbled...
he moaned...
he fumbled...

he groaned.

like a pair of clipped wings
his frail arms struggled to spread out
as if chained in thousand strings
gripping up his psyche fast in their clout.

from the front pocket, he pulled out the cellphone;
from another pocket, he drew out his credit cards;
from the pants' pocket, he took out the pink slip;
from the same pocket, he pulled out the car keys;
and veritably offered them to the still, stinking river,
slowly murmuring, "i'm coming into your lap, too."

puffing out the pungent breath scornfully,
and preparing to become another victim
of the river's snares he shut the moist eyelids,
then jerked and sobbed
and smirked and propped
"let me have the last laugh.
none can call me names past this moment:
i'm not a moron, mad and horribly hollow.
let me forego these titles forever!
choices made in the past haunt my present.
they shall not trouble my future.
the tunnel of freedom is laid through the waters beneath.
i promise not to return, to disturb and to breathe"
stared he down at the crinkling surface one last time
thought of the mother who'd blessed him with sunshine.

finally another man was ready to jump into the river;
once again nobody would care nor would quiver.
how many men would refuse to fight and give up;
will an angel enlighten 'em and make 'em live up?
life must continue even without the prized possessions;
empty flamboyance only leads to soul's repressions.

ii

the inviolable *vayu*

echoes of the crowd still rang in her heart.
what was that pain that refused to depart?
someone's victory had left her aghast.
couldn't she let it go and improve her craft?

no, the loss was very heavy; and it ripped her apart.
the acrid memory lived on and whipped her apart.
with time, her self-evoked pain became even worse,
the silly student did nothing but prepared her hearse.

post the failure, she'd dawdle under the gnarled tree
despised she every well-wisher who told her to agree,
to the situation that shattered the castle of her hopes.
her love too advised her to move on, but she yelled '*nopes*!'

siloed by something uncanny, she lived like the zombies do,
did she talk to wild apparitions who, around her, often flew?
how long would she wander the aimless alleys?
who'd dare to get her out of these lightless galleys?

ye fragile beauty, your lamentation is a trivial exercise
one must be prompt to abandon this and struggle to rise.
webbed in the fatal illusions of your broken dreams
you'd be a prisoner but of your weird notions, it seems.

finally that day was around when everyone went home
but she was happy alone staying in the hostel room.
'i can't go home and face parents," often she hummed
'that was my last chance,' this thought had her numbed.

troubled by wretched memories in the silence of corridors
i'd discover answers for my ugly loss, she was damn'd sure.
but someone with a heart of stone did always refuse
coaxing her to tuck the head right in the nylon noose.

here was a moment of misery that got stuck in time
neither did she have a second nor she willed to unwind.
in a quick succession she arranged her altar under the fan
and finally stood draped on the stool in a very short span

"come, hug me, ye death, and free me of the slur.
do i not have the right to go where the rest does blur?"
bewildered and wired to the ceiling, her lips did purse;
in a conflict with herself, she got eaten by the strange curse.

echoes of the crowd still rang in her heart.
what was this pain that refused to depart?
someone's victory had left her aghast.
couldn't she let it go and focus on her craft?

iii
the sacred *prithvi*

in his red-rimmed eyes did glint the pain of ages
his famished physique looked as if famished sages
angry at the land's nothingness, he trudged up
frustrated at the neck-breaking years he'd drudged up
in the fields inherited from forefathers,
in the fields that ruined him and many others.

thus he went up until the extreme end of the cliff
stared he down shivering but didn't even sniff
emptiness and silence lay deep in the ravine.
will it give him peace like no other shrine?
his step, he knew, would leave his family shaken;
but the poor farmer is firm at the decision he's taken.

from the end of the impervious hill, he gazed down
from the end of his wits, he pitied the village brown—
the canvass of his hamlet appears sterile and without scope
that robbed them of everything including the thought of hope:

leafless trees
dried wells

dusty terraced fields
dying cattle
scrawny tillers
and smoke billowing
from in-between the pine trees...

tears streamed down his sunken cheeks
as he crashed down on his knees
"o duds, don't work like the drunken freaks.
there's no good coming your way.
the rain-divorced land will not yield!
the rain-divorced land can not yield!"

"my arms have run out of strength!
i deride, i spit, i loathe thy hazy skulls!"
advanced he to the ledge of the cliff,
ahead of which was a pool of air
bottomed with a craggy rockbed down below
in the dark, shrubby ravine where nocturnals dwell.
he closed the rheumy eyes unsatisfactorily,
chucked the worn-out cellphone grimacing
and stuck the last beedi between his cleft lips...

iv

the mystical *akash*

water stirred with bubbles blue
choked man's breaths rolled out and flew;
the soul was still trapped in the quagmire
stinking in the sewage that spat fire.
may the rains come early and dissolve this sludge!
may the deceased rest in peace sans the grudge!

self-strangulated, and
caught in snares of death,
the diva swayed stuck in the cord;
the stool clinked on the floor;
a speck of dust sprang up from the taut string;
a muffled squeak waned in the hostel corridors
with hands fluttering
and legs scuttling
groundless... wriggling in the air.

cradled in the blood-soaked rocks
slept his rammed, mangled physique.
the air zoomed past

ruffling the gray locks,
singing a rueful symphony
and chasing the insatiated spirit away
through the rock-bed
and on to the gates of eternity.

v

the purifying *agni*

across the waters purple
across the sky grey
across the earth arid
ah! shackled in thoughts surreal
indecisive minds opt for their burial.
let the waters cleanse them up
and set them right without the trends
on the shores of the endless skies;
millions of miles south of earth
where the hope of hope and peace
are believed to persist permanently
and where the air smells of jasmine.

traffic continues unabated on the bridge in broad daylight.
silence continues to echo down the hostel corridors.
peasants continue to till the dead hillside.

stinking carcasses are finally smelt and recovered
then surrounded, lamented and forever covered.

let them pass through the fires red.
let them be counted amid the cowards and the dead.

The Last Cigarette

shall i run away from the madding noise and live in recluse?
shall i sell my house, my car and every prized possession?
shall i steal from the neighbour's chest and further bemuse?
shall i rob a bank or rush to a place to douse my obsession?

with no solution in sight, how do i repay my lenders?
shall i kill my wife, my kids and bury their dreams forever?
shall i rid 'em of the painful future that's flooded with reminders?
or shall i jump into the arabian and dissolve in its tidal fervor?

standing between this world and the limitless water pool
i must have but one last cigarette to rewind what i've been through
wow! this moment of flashbacks still makes me drool
bhagwan! do i still have options? can everything still unscrew?

'one more time, one more time,' i glance at the smoked butt.
'one more time, one more time,' i take a step back.
'one more time, one more time,' i will clear the borrowed glut.
'one more time, one more time,' i have the confidence i lack.

Live-In No More

more than the prison bars, your lie incinerates me.
more than the court judgment, your conviction berates me.
more than the incendiary press, your demeanor lacerates me.
more than the voices around, your accusation shakes me.

what stirred you to call my fondness an act of rape?
what forced you to embark upon such an act of escape?
what tempted you to libel the sanctity of our loving grace?
what prompted you to call me a piece of that unsocial race?

didn't i offer you endless bouquets of tulips and roses?
didn't we go to the movies and kiss among the fragrant posies?
how about those pilgrimages, holidays and excursions
that we've had together without caring about aspersions?

what will you achieve if i am thrown in prison?
what will you achieve if i languish there in every season?
what's my fault, my crime? have i done a treason?
thought of this day never even in my distant vision.

huh! wish me inner peace, and a life sans thy morbid mist.
pray for me so that i can get over this grotesque twist.
i didn't know our love story had an entirely altered script
but i promise to return thy courtesy, but with my slit wrist.

Woman In The Metro
at the hauz khas metro station

a glimpse of the woman unknown does to me
what an oasis does to a parched traveller
in the desert.
she's a blink in the eye.
she's the glimmer in the sky.
she's my co-commuter.
she's my love; i her suitor.
i see her every morning and in the evenings too.
but she becomes quicksand whenever i decide to woo.

is she an illusion—
my mind's wildest confusion?
why does she stand close to me but not utter a word?
there's something eerie about her that's left me stirred.
tomorrow i'll surely ask her name—
and get a selfie in my cell's frame.
what if she refutes or says *no*
should i move on and farther row?
a glimpse of the woman unknown...
a glimpse of the woman g...

ii
the other day at the hauz khas station

a glimpse of the woman unknown does to me
what a blooming flower does to a honey bee
in the wildest heath.
she is the princess of my dreams
she is a smile amid grisly screams
she's the symphony that stops clamor
she's the gentle shower that ends summer
her image tricks me like an ingenious con
whenever i try to touch her, she's gone.

is she an apparition—
roaming in desperation?
her appearance seems lugging the sadness of ages
only seen at the metro, she's a garden full of daisies.
o no! why she's jumping on the underground track
while stopping her i too land down with a sudden
smack.
'why didn't the train hurt me and run me over?
hear this hysteria? is it me in that gurney cover?'

the woman unknown is finally mine
i be dead, it has been her design.
she and i now will work together
to soak metro tracks forever
with the blood of disturbed folks
whom the society often mocks.

a glimpse of the woman unknown...
a glimpse of the woman gone...

Sensitive Mind

trouble brews deep on the battle turf of her psyche;
a horde of hooligans is heard marching closer;
their sinister designs put her heart to pace;
their notorious arsenal churns and spews fury.

grisly thoughts take on, multiplying anxiety and fear;
the attempts to rein in on adverse ideations fail
as warring tribes wound the walls of her cranium.
she digs her head in the pillow whimpering.

locusts and hornets attack to nail her down;
the only way out is to put everything to rest
by pouring kerosene on the head and lighting it up
to char the dreadful thoughts once and for all.

repeatedly she attempts it so that
the tumultuous mind may return to calmness.

Blown And Hopeless

the songs are gone
the symphonies are blown
the cacophony captures
amid the phantasmal raptures

the trust is broken
the faith is shaken
the din holds me fast
on to that point at last

the hate is up
the love is low
the return is hopeless
into the commotion, scope-less

Suicide Pact:
Killed Children Demand Answers

burning like the fires red
and speaking of the souls dead
my brother and i will haunt you
until you answer us, won't you?
why did you kill us?
why did you kill us?

killed us like we aren't your blood
maimed us in sleep like the hapless buds
but, we'll chase you even in death
until you tell why you stopped our breath
why did you kill us?
why did you kill us?

we'd have lived with your suicide
had you thought of us and let us decide
but no, your business plans were screwed
gone were your assets you'd accrued.
why did you kill us?
why did you kill us?

Chaotic Self

calm amid chaos
cheerful amid loss
she keeps hushing
and forcefully pressing
a swarm of thoughts
that she has fought
since times unknown
in her head alone.

living even though
she wants to die.
stoic even though
she wants to cry.

Good Bye, Mom!

i'm the cactus of your life's desert.
even if my thorns have hurt you
i am the only greenery you've seen.
but now on, our path has forked:
yours goes into the earthly noise;
mine calls me up into the celestial cradle.
i cannot lug the weight
of your hopes and my failures
beyond this point.
good bye, mom!

Water Of A Pond

i am the water of a pond, right now
squirming to blend with a river, but how?
this pond keeps me shackled
in issues that i haven't tackled
like they expect me to in months or years.
it feels as if i'm drowning in a sea of tears.

through the river flowing
and into the limitless seas glowing
away from this corporeal bond
where exists no commotion and no sound
i want to experience the loveliness of divine light
i want to experience the beauty of eternal delight

will i have my entrapped soul ever released?
will i have my shackled whole ever unleashed
from the chains of flesh and bones
from the hues of earth and stones?
will i stop to feel the pain and passion?
will i stop to erode in fears of death and depression?

Before I Met You

before i saw you at the bookstore on a monsoon day
i was nothing but a bulb without the electric wire
clouded in dust and shrouded in ignominy
unable to beat the night cover—my sworn enemy

before you hit me like the light at the end of the tunnel
i whirled around like a rusty fan in dizzying circles
you gave me both a purpose and a direction
and fired in me both - emotions and erection.

before your warm breasts set off my volcano of passion
i was like a ruined garden in the smart city of joy
you ignited in me the velocity of a bullet train
and prompted my love like the sprays of grain.

before you lay bare by my side emitting that sexy odor
i felt like a cellphone that had no sim and no signal
ambling unknowingly on paths that went nowhere
and straying in the stinking delhi lanes without the fresh air.

will you take me away from this unending season of sadness?
will you touch me, kiss me and hug me again?

Good Bye

the thought of goodbye does to my heart
what oil does to fire.
it burns in longing
and singes in desire.

the whiff of not seeing you back again
sucks me into a deadwood
lain in a dank, unnoticed corner
where i'll breathe last in all likelihood.

The Last Words

please feed moti on time so it doesn't die.
please water the plants so they don't dry
please open the piggy bank when i'm gone
please get yourself an iphone from amazon
to my lovely sis, that's my last gift
i hope you'll forgive me for every ugly rift
please take care of ma and pa as they're old
please ignore the hot words that i've told
now i've a long journey ahead
away from this earth and into the dead.

That Kiss You Stole

the first kiss you stole on the staircase left me insane.
neither had i a throb nor a movement in the brain.
transfixed and numb, i felt as if i was in another land.
stirred and feverish, i was a zombie half-sunk in sand.

that current of a thousand bolts still electrifies the memory
nudging me into nostalgic insobriety. hm, such a sweet reverie!
the magical touch of those puckered lips was a scintillating start
but where did you disappear suddenly? it burns my heart.

show up at least to return me that kiss...

Let My Journey Be My Destination

when the destined place is all in the eye and seems closer
i should be dancing on toes but am underwhelmed like a loser.
my heart mourns and shrinks in size
my legs swell so as not to let me arrive.
let my journey be my destination

i don't know what intrigues me so much about the journey;
why the awareness of its cessation throws me on the gurney
chained and shackled i refuse to reach
'don't end, ay, so soon,' i piously beseech.
let my journey be my destination

when that turn of the travel nears the last resort
the feeling of being caught in a vortex begins to retort
i feel like i'm dying on the slopes
and commiting suicide sans the hopes.
let my journey be my destination

The Lovely You

like every highrise seems to lure me to the terrace
your lens-studded eyes lure me to steal you from your beau

like every narrow valley seems to entice me to the spooky ravines
your lush, satin lips provoke me to snatch you from your partner

like every treacherous pass tempts me to the fatal elegance
your burly breasts tempt me to eliminate 'em all and marry you

in you, i see a road passing through the gardens of pink flowers
in you, i hear the music of guzzling rivers, brooks and waterfalls

without you, the life is a war-torn turf infested with scoundrels
without you, i'm a brakeless truck willing to destroy everyone

Strange Woman Of The Highway

alone on the open road
in love with the music of wheels
thinking of the golden days ahead
i continue to steer forward on long-hauls
it's just one hope
it's just one thing
it's you, ay pretty lady
i've seen you follow me on the highway

no more like a throwaway potato
an indifferent fan of the quirky roads
confident of a relaxing life together
i continue to accelerate to fulfil my dreams
it's just one hope
it's just one thing
it's you, ay pretty lady
i've seen you stare at me on the highway

along my journeys of miles
by crossing this cabbie's paths
and smiling through your white gown
you've sparked heat into my cold embers

it's just one hope
it's just one thing
it's you, ay mysterious lady
i've seen you turn me crazy at the wild turns

who're you, ay, strange woman on these highway turns?
i wish you'd touch me, rub me and take me in your arms!
but i heard once a veteran say a secret in my ear:
death is as charming as you, ay, my fair deception.

Deaf Ears

the wobbling wheel in the speeding car
prods the riders persistently
but warnings fall on the deaf ears.
will dilating eyes at the reckoning hour
help those - drunk and dreaming?

Cocaine Queen

ads of curvaceous chicks on top-end billboards
bombard me with a shower of shooting stones.
once industry's most celebrated model, i am
now a despicable and forgotten cocaine queen.
memories scathe and reality burns me with jealousy!

A Jilted Bitch

astride an arrogant horse i played but
a jilted bitch to rein in his frisking mind.
but the more i tried the more he drifted away.
his callousness makes me realise that
my search to seek meaning in life
was like discovering music in commotion,
salt in sand and water in parched land.

Postscript

Feelings of suicide are universal. But a majority of humans are able to overpower them by simply engaging in regular chores and endeavoring to search peace in disquietness, hope in despair and order in chaos. I have had my share of such feelings, too. Most of my suicidal feelings appeared feeble and did not last long in front of my determination and my habit of searching for positive in negative and light in the darkness. But there is a memory of one such feeling that still haunts me. It had been a feeling whose vibration makes me numb even today. It emerged from a horrible experience. An experience that everyone wants only his sworn enemy to go through. It was a time when I was appearing in the final board exams of the 10th standard. Excitement and perplexity subjugated my psyche. In the month of March with spring flowers blooming all around in the hilly district – Hamirpur – of Himachal Pradesh, I was worried and was thinking of ways to pass exams.

The exam center was not in the school I was enrolled in but a few miles away in another school. We had to walk past many villages, through wheat-laden fields, slopy tracts and forests to reach the center. It is not that our village was devoid of a motorable road. But buses were rare in those days and drove at odd hours. Personal vehicles were highly expensive; the rich could only afford.

The phobia of the 10th exams gripped me tight. *Passing the matriculation exam is as hard as climbing to the tip of Mount Everest*, everyone including my teachers, friends and relatives had preached million times. Whosoever passed matriculation in one go or without failing would garner praise from relatives, neighbours and villagers. This had instilled in me a fear that you had to be either super-intelligent or cheat in the exams. I counted myself amongst the average so cheating was the only saviour. Moreover cheating, in those days, was considered a pious act as opposed to failing. Everyone did it vehemently and proudly. A few students would even post their aides outside the exam hall so that they could hurl answer chits through door chinks, wall holes and broken window panes. No one opposed. Nor even the examiner.

My exams started on a resounding note. I attempted all questions – even the ones I had no clue about in the initial papers, thanks to the teachers who allowed mass cheating. *Why should one work hard if we can pass so easily?* I convinced myself. School-sponsored repugnance in the initial few papers drugged my mind so intensely that I even forgot to differentiate between good and bad, and stopped looking at books afterwards for the rest of the papers.

But only until that day. It was the most important paper – mathematics. Most feared math very much and would fail miserably. However, having looked at the question paper, I was ecstatic since I didn't feel the need to pull the hidden stuff out. I could easily solve intricate problems.

But then, all of a sudden, a flying squad sent by the Himachal Pradesh Board of School Education invaded the center. Several students found cheating landed in their net. I was one of them, even though I was not cheating. They had searched through my pockets and discovered one.

What ensued later is inexplicable. Extreme guilt, shame, fear, loneliness, hopelessness, worthlessness and despair surrounded me. Not to mention, everyone in the known circles was deploring me and trying to cross all limits of ill-talk. No one had ever been caught cheating in the village before. Filled with contrition, I felt destroyed and ruined. The School Board was about to bar me for three years from appearing in any exam. The impending punishment meant nothing more than the end of the road. It was then that I wanted to face no one. Thoughts of suicide began to fetter and encroach upon me steadily. I wished to be dead, invisible, run over by an unruly truck or washed away by a roaring river. With no desire to move on, I strayed in empty corners and remained isolated from friends. It was one of the worst phases of my life and perhaps the first that involved truckloads of guilt and shame.

Days went by. Believing that the entire world wanted to destroy me, I kept locked in my room.

But then I realized that I was perhaps overreacting to the situation by overburdening myself with unnecessary fears and wretched thoughts. Nobody gave a damn about me. I noticed that self-imposed curfew was futile and worthless. I fired up the animal spirit within and persuaded myself to face fearlessly everything that came what may (even the three-year ban).

I simply didn't want to be stuck in time while everyone around was moving forward. Thus, I got involved frequently with friends and family members. I took their jibes and ill-commentary constructively. In fact, I was the one to scold and call myself an idiot, before they did whenever I sensed a circumstance of that kind arising. As a result, soon the thoughts of dying vanished like quicksand. I was poised for a fresh start.

Let me divulge to you that I got another chance to appear in the mathematics exam after six months. There was no three years ban imposed, not even a year lost. And the rest is history.

ONKAR SHARMA is a senior business technology journalist with more than 15 years of experience across publications. He is former editor of Dataquest (DQIndia.com), India's leading IT magazine, and Voice&Data (voicendata.com), India's leading telecom magazine. In his current role at a Big Four firm, he is principal consultant of cyber security. Onkar also edits and manages an e-journal, LiteraryYard.com, where short stories, essays and poems from all over the world on different themes and topics are published.

www.ingramcontent.com/pod-product-compliance
Lightning Source LLC
LaVergne TN
LVHW090026180726
843489LV00008B/3016